INFIDELITY AND FORGIVENESS

Rebuilding Trust And Coping With Infidelity Through Forgiveness

By

ADELE ROOSEVELT

Copyright © Adele Roosevelt
May 2023.

All rights reserved.

TABLE OF CONTENTS

Introduction 3

Infidelity as it Implies 5

Why People Cheat? 6

Ways infidelity can take form 7

Rebuilding and Repairing the Damage 22

Forgiving Infidelity, Adultery, 31

Separation and Divorce 31

Introduction

Infidelity is a painful and devastating experience that can test even the strongest of relationships. Whether it is a one-time mistake or an ongoing affair, the betrayal of trust can leave both partners feeling hurt, angry, and unsure of the future. However, while infidelity can cause irreparable damage, it is not always the end of a relationship. Many couples choose to work through the pain and rebuild their relationship, creating a stronger bond that can withstand future challenges.

Rebuilding trust after cheating is a complex and challenging process that requires both partners to be committed to repairing the relationship. Forgiveness plays a crucial role in this process, but it is not a quick fix. It requires time, patience, and a willingness to communicate and work through difficult emotions. In this context, forgiveness does not mean forgetting or excusing the infidelity, but rather choosing to move forward and create a new, stronger foundation of trust.

In this book, we will explore the intricacies of infidelity and the process of rebuilding trust after cheating. We will discuss the emotional impact of infidelity, the challenges of forgiveness, and the practical steps that couples can take to repair their relationship. Drawing on research, case studies, and personal experiences, this book aims to provide a comprehensive guide for couples who are struggling to rebuild their relationship after infidelity. Whether you are the betrayed partner or the one who cheated, this book is designed to help you navigate the difficult journey of healing and rebuilding trust.

Infidelity as it Implies

Infidelity, also referred to as cheating, involves disregarding the promises, agreements, and commitments made with one's partner and betraying their trust. Essentially, it involves breaking the rules of a relationship. Although the typical definition of infidelity assumes that individuals have previously discussed and established boundaries in their relationship, many people fail to do so.

However, it's still possible to be unfaithful, even without prior discussions. For example, if someone feels the need to keep something hidden from their partner or engages in behaviors they wouldn't do in their partner's presence; it's a sign of crossing a line in the relationship. Similarly, if one directs their attention and energy to someone or something other than their partner, they are likely being unfaithful.

Why People Cheat?

Learning that your partner has been unfaithful can be an overwhelming experience, evoking a range of emotions such as hurt, anger, sadness, and even physical distress. The burning question of "Why?" may consume your thoughts, yet the answer is often complex and multifaceted.

Infidelity can stem from a variety of reasons, including unfulfilled needs or unresolved issues within the romantic or sexual relationship. On the other hand, it may also be a result of the cheater's personal traumas, feelings, or needs that are unaddressed or unidentified. For instance, a fear of commitment or witnessing a parent's infidelity in childhood may lead someone to cheat on their partner.

However, it's crucial to note that even if a partner's infidelity is a result of unresolved issues within the relationship, it is not the fault of the other partner, and it does not mean that they are inadequate. To emphasize, if you have been cheated on, it's not your fault.

For example, if one partner is frequently occupied with work, the other partner may feel emotionally or physically neglected. However, if the neglected partner turns to someone else, it does not necessarily mean that the other partner is responsible for their infidelity. It only implies that there was an unmet need that required attention. Regrettably, instead of addressing it with their partner, they strayed.

Ways infidelity can take form

When the term "infidelity" is mentioned, one may immediately envision a person being unfaithful by engaging in sexual acts with someone other than their spouse or concealing a sexual relationship from their partner.

Infidelity, in its essence, refers to any violation of the agreed-upon interpersonal dynamic within a pre-established romantic relationship. Although infidelity is commonly associated with physical acts, such as engaging in sexual activity with someone other than one's partner when there is an agreement for sexual exclusivity, it is not solely limited to sexual infidelity. Infidelity can be a breach of any emotional, romantic, or intellectual agreement made with one's committed romantic and/or sexual partner. Romantic, emotional, intellectual, and even cyber cheating are all types of infidelity, emphasizing that cheating is not always limited to sexual involvement.

In summary, we have explored various forms and manifestations of infidelity beyond the commonly perceived sexual context.

1. **Sexual Infidelity:** is often the first thing that comes to mind when people hear the term "infidelity." This type of betrayal covers a wide range of activities, from secret hotel trysts and flings to engaging in virtual sex via social media platforms or even touching someone's foot under the table during a dinner party.
It's a common misconception that only people in monogamous relationships can be guilty of sexual infidelity. In fact, people in any type of relationship can be unfaithful sexually.

2. **Emotional infidelity:** is often referred to as non-physical cheating, and it involves developing intimate emotional connections outside of one's committed relationship. However, the term can be problematic as it promotes the outdated notion that people can only have emotional connections with their spouse. It's important to acknowledge that individuals can and should have meaningful connections with others outside of their relationship(s).

Nonetheless, emotional cheating is a real phenomenon and can be just as harmful, if not more so, than physical infidelity. The distinction between a close platonic friendship and emotional unfaithfulness lies in the presence of secrecy or desire.

Emotional infidelity occurs when one diverts their emotional energy away from their partner and towards someone else. This involves actively choosing to focus attention and efforts on the other person, rather than simply seeking support from them as a friend. It can also involve expressing deep feelings of desire, love, or longing to someone other than one's partner. While emotional infidelity can take many forms, it often includes confiding in a third party about relationship issues instead of discussing them with one's partner. It may also involve celebrating personal achievements with a coworker, while downplaying them to one's partner. In more extreme cases, emotional infidelity may involve falling for someone else, expressing romantic interest in them, or excessively complimenting them to the point of hurting one's partner. All of these behaviors could potentially lead to physical infidelity as well.

3. **Romantic infidelity:** occurs when you engage in behaviors commonly associated with romance, such as flirting, wining and dining, and building emotional connections, with someone other than your partner. However, the definition of what constitutes romance may differ from person to person.

Although there is considerable overlap between romantic and emotional infidelity, romantic infidelity is typically characterized by actions taken with another person, while emotional infidelity is characterized by feelings directed toward another person.

4. **Intellectual Infidelity:** When a couple shares similar beliefs regarding communication, politics, values, intellectual pursuits, or interests, they are considered to be intellectually compatible. While it is normal to have common interests with people other than your partner, if you direct your attention and energy towards a third party exclusively, it could be viewed as a form of cheating. This could qualify as intellectual infidelity if you start avoiding discussing certain topics with your partner because you prefer discussing them with someone else.

Similarly, if you start a new TV show with someone other than your partner, it could be problematic. While having hobbies and interests with other people is fine, the important thing to keep in mind is that if you find someone else more intellectually stimulating than your partner, it could lead to intellectual infidelity.

5. **Cyber-Cheating on Social Media:** Cyber-cheating, which is also referred to as digital infidelity or engaging in a cyber-affair, involves infidelity that takes place exclusively through online channels such as social media and text messaging. Nowadays, many people use cyber affairs as a way to stray from their partners or to test the waters of infidelity without feeling like they have committed actual cheating. Rather than rendezvousing at a hotel for a quick tryst during their lunch break, modern unfaithful partners may exchange explicit media or spend hours conversing on platforms like Facebook or Snapchat.

It is important to understand that cyber-cheating does not necessarily involve sexual content, although it may involve suggestive messages of that nature. In the context of a relationship, cyber-cheating can consist of actions such as sending someone a good morning text, phoning them while on the way home from work to talk about your day, or sharing pictures via text. However, it should be noted that these behaviors may also be indicative of emotional cheating. As you may have already realized, there is significant overlap between various types of infidelity, and it is not uncommon for multiple forms of cheating to occur simultaneously.

Once more, the issue is with the violation of the agreements made within your relationship. Thus, if you engage with an individual online or via your mobile device who falls outside the boundaries of your relationship agreements, it could be regarded as a form of cyber infidelity.

In 2017, The Journal of Sex Research published a study aimed at examining the reasons behind infidelity in romantic relationships. The study employed an online survey that queried 495 individuals who had engaged in cheating behavior.

Of the participants, 259 were female, 213 were male, and 23 did not specify their gender. The majority identified as mostly heterosexual (87.9%) and were primarily young adults (with an average age of 20 years), with just over half reporting being in some form of romantic relationship.

The study identified eight main factors that drive infidelity, although it is important to note that these factors do not account for all instances of cheating. Nonetheless, they offer a useful framework for gaining a deeper understanding of why individuals may cheat in relationships.

Here are the eight key factors and how they may manifest in a relationship:

i. Anger
ii. Falling out of love
iii. Situation/Opportunity
iv. Commitment issues
v. Unmet needs
vi. Desire
vii. Variety
viii. Self-esteem

It is important to note that these factors are not exhaustive, and each individual case of infidelity may be influenced by a variety of unique factors. Nonetheless, these categories offer insight into some of the common reasons that may contribute to cheating in romantic relationships.

1. **Anger/Retribution:** Infidelity may occur due to anger or a desire for retribution. For instance, discovering that one's partner has cheated can be a shocking and painful experience that may prompt the desire to make them experience the same feelings. This form of infidelity is often retaliatory and is motivated by the idea of "they hurt me, so now I'll hurt them."

However, anger-based infidelity may not always be about revenge and may also be driven by other factors, such as:

i. Feelings of anger or frustration after an argument with a partner.

ii. Resentment towards a partner who is frequently absent.

iii. Frustration towards a partner who is unable to provide physical or emotional support.

iv. Dissatisfaction with a relationship in which a partner seems to lack understanding of one's needs.

In all cases, anger can be a compelling force that pushes individuals to seek emotional or physical intimacy with someone other than their partner.

2. **Falling out of love:** The initial rush of falling in love with someone often wanes with time. Although stable, long-lasting love can exist, the excitement and passion that accompany the early stages of a relationship tend to diminish.

Once the honeymoon phase is over, you may come to the realization that the love between you and your partner is no longer there, or that you've fallen in love with someone else.

However, even when romantic love fades, it can be difficult to leave a relationship that provides a sense of family, friendship, stability, and safety. Remaining in such a relationship without the presence of romantic love can result in a desire to experience love again, which may motivate individuals to engage in infidelity.

3. **Situation/Opportunity:** Infidelity becomes more likely when a person has the opportunity to

cheat, although not everyone who has such an opportunity would engage in cheating. Other factors may also contribute to the motivation to cheat. For instance, imagine a scenario where a person is experiencing a sense of low self-esteem due to their appearance and is also feeling a lack of connection in their current relationship. In this situation, if a coworker expresses attraction towards the person, they may be more likely to cheat as a result of the combination of these motivating factors.

In addition to these factors, there are certain situational factors that can increase the likelihood of infidelity, even in an otherwise strong and fulfilling relationship. Examples of such factors include:

i. Residing or working in a setting where there is a significant amount of physical contact and emotional bonding, such as a military unit or a religious community
ii. Seeking physical comfort and intimacy with another person following a traumatic or upsetting event.

iii. Consuming excessive amounts of alcohol and engaging in sexual activity with someone after a night out.

4. **Commitment issues:** Infidelity can also be motivated by commitment issues. Commitment means different things to different people and those who struggle with commitment may be more likely to cheat. Two partners may have different ideas about the relationship status or level of commitment, such as whether it's casual or exclusive.

Even if a person really likes their partner, they may fear making a commitment to them. In such cases, cheating might be seen as a way to avoid commitment, even if they would prefer to stay in the relationship.

Other reasons for commitment-related infidelity include a lack of interest in committing long-term, wanting a more casual relationship, or wanting a way out of a relationship.

5. **Unmet needs:** In some relationships, one or both partners may not have their needs for intimacy met, which can lead to frustration. Despite the relationship being fulfilling in other aspects, they may choose to remain hopeful that the situation will improve. However, if the situation persists, the frustration may intensify and provide motivation to seek fulfillment elsewhere.

There are various reasons for unmet needs, including sexual needs. This may happen when:

i. One or both partners frequently spend time apart from each other.
ii. The partners have mismatched sex drives.
iii. One partner may have physical limitations preventing them from having sex or may have lost interest in sexual activities.

6. **Sexual desire:** The desire for sex alone can be a motivating factor for some people to cheat. While other factors such as opportunity and unmet sexual needs may contribute to infidelity, a simple desire for sexual activity may be enough for some individuals to seek it outside of their committed relationship.

Even individuals in relationships with fulfilling sexual experiences may still desire sex with others. This desire could be attributed to a high level of sexual drive rather than any problems with their current relationship.

7. **Desire for variety:** In a relationship, some individuals may crave variety, particularly when it comes to sexual experiences. For instance, someone might want to experiment with different sexual practices that their partner may not be interested in, even if they have a good match in other aspects of the relationship.

Craving variety can also extend to other areas, such as:

i.   Diverse conversations or communication styles.
ii. Different non-sexual activities.
iii. Developing relationships with other people in addition to their current partner.

Attraction to others is another factor that contributes to the desire for variety. People can be attracted to various types of individuals, and this attraction may not cease just because they are in a committed relationship. Some people in monogamous relationships may struggle to resist acting on their attraction towards others.

8. **Low Self-esteem:** Infidelity can sometimes be motivated by low self-esteem. Individuals who engage in cheating may seek a boost to their self-esteem by having sex with a new partner, which can lead to feelings of empowerment, attractiveness, confidence, and success.

Even if the person has a loving and supportive partner who offers compassion and encouragement, they may still feel that their partner is obligated to do so or may doubt the sincerity of their compliments. In contrast, receiving admiration and approval from someone new can be more exciting and seem more genuine to someone with low self-esteem, who may believe that the new person has no relationship obligation to lie or exaggerate.

Rebuilding and Repairing the Damage

One significant finding from this study is that infidelity is frequently not related to the other person involved.

Although many individuals who cheat may love their partners and harbor no intention of causing harm, they may still endeavor to conceal their infidelity from their partners. However, such behavior can inflict considerable harm to a relationship.

The act of cheating does not necessarily signify the termination of a relationship, but rebuilding and progressing forward require effort.

In the event that your partner has engaged in infidelity:

The discovery can leave you feeling overwhelmed and unsure of how to proceed. You might be contemplating ways to mend the relationship, or you may have already decided to end it.

If you find yourself unsure of what to do next, consider the following suggestions:

i. It is advisable to have a conversation with your partner regarding the infidelity, and it may be helpful to involve a couples therapist or a neutral third party in the discussion. While understanding your partner's motivations can assist in making an informed decision, it is generally recommended to refrain from delving into the specific details of the encounter.

ii. Inquire whether your partner desires to sustain the relationship. It is critical to understand their sentiments as some individuals may resort to infidelity as a way of ending the relationship.

iii. Evaluate whether you can regain trust in your partner. Rebuilding trust can be a gradual process, and your partner may recognize this. However, if you are certain that you can never trust them again, it is unlikely that the relationship can be salvaged.

iv. Question your own desire to maintain the relationship. Evaluate whether you genuinely love your partner and are willing to address any underlying problems, or if you are simply apprehensive about starting a new relationship. Consider if the relationship is worth mending.

v. Consider seeking the guidance of a counselor. While couples therapy is strongly recommended when working on a relationship post-infidelity, individual therapy can also aid in sorting through your emotions and thoughts regarding the situation.

If you've cheated on your partner:

If you have engaged in infidelity, it is crucial to contemplate your motives carefully and have a sincere conversation with your partner. Your partner may or may not be interested in reconciling the relationship, and it is essential to respect their decision, regardless of your own desire to salvage the relationship.

Allocate some time for reflection on the following points:

i. Are you still committed to the relationship? If your infidelity stemmed from a desire to end the relationship, it is advisable to be upfront with your partner about it. If you are unsure of your motivations, working with a therapist may provide you with some clarity.

ii. Can you address the underlying reasons for the infidelity? Engaging in individual or couples therapy and enhancing communication can aid in improving the relationship and reducing the likelihood of future infidelity. However, if you cheated due to your partner's lack of interest in a particular sexual preference or their prolonged absence, what steps would you take if a similar situation arises in the future? Would you be able to have an open dialogue with your partner about your desire to cheat rather than engaging in infidelity?

iii. Do you anticipate engaging in infidelity again? Cheating can cause significant emotional distress, pain, and heartbreak. If you have concerns about engaging in infidelity again, avoid making a false promise of faithfulness to your partner. Instead, it may be more appropriate to be honest with them about your reservations and communicate that you may not be able to commit.

iv. Are you willing to make a commitment to attend therapy?

In conclusion, the common phrase "Once a cheater, always a cheater" may not necessarily apply to everyone as some individuals may cheat only once. It's worth noting that going through the process of addressing infidelity can potentially improve and reinforce the relationship.

However, honesty and open communication are vital for both partners to determine what is and is not feasible to commit to in the relationship. Moving forward, maintaining transparency with each other is critical to ensure the relationship is healthy and sustainable.

A relationship can survive infidelity, and these processes can help:

1. **Earning back trust and re-establishing trust** are essential after infidelity. Essentially, cheating breaks trust in a relationship, and rebuilding trust requires effort from both partners. However, the steps required may differ from one relationship to another.

To regain trust, the partner who cheated should be willing to sever contact with the person they had an affair with. Additionally, they need to be ready to take the following actions to rebuild their partner's trust:

i. Communicate with their partner if the person they cheated with contacts them again.
ii. Inform their partner about their whereabouts and company in the future.
iii. Maintain transparency regarding their phone, social media accounts, and other devices.
iv. Be understanding of their partner's need to verify things initially.

2. To move forward from infidelity, it's important for all parties involved to consciously make a decision to leave the past pain behind and create space for a new kind of connection. While the person who cheated needs to earn their partner's trust and the partner who was cheated on may have specific needs and requests to feel safe again, there must be room for re-connecting and turning over a new leaf.

One strategy to achieve this is to set aside 15 minutes each day for acknowledging anger, emotions, and inquiries about the affair, while investing the rest of the time in quality time, connection, and even having fun together. This deliberate investment of time is a way to move towards healing and creating a new future.

3. **Obtaining the assistance of a couple's therapist** is essential when dealing with the aftermath of infidelity. The aftermath of an affair can shake the foundation of a relationship and many couples struggle to repair the damage. It is important to work with a couple's therapist who

has expertise in infidelity and cheating to help facilitate the healing process.

4. **Working with an individual therapist** in addition to a couple's therapist can be beneficial in dealing with the aftermath of infidelity. While couples therapy can help both partners work through the betrayal, individual therapy can help each person assess whether they are willing to put in the effort to repair the relationship. It can also assist the partner who cheated in examining any underlying beliefs about love and fidelity that may have contributed to their behavior. Furthermore, if the relationship cannot be salvaged, individual therapy can provide guidance on ending the relationship in a practical and emotionally healthy way.

5. **Demonstrate your love every day from now on.** Love is an action that requires continuous effort to sustain. True healing from infidelity starts when all partners begin to show their love every single day.

To act with love, consider asking yourself these questions and let your answers guide your actions:

i. What actions can I take today to demonstrate my love for my partner?
ii. What actions can I take today to make my partner feel attractive and desirable?
iii. How can I demonstrate to my partner that I am committed to our relationship and the agreements we have made?

In conclusion, infidelity can manifest in various forms, each equally distressing and painful. However, if the parties involved are committed to the process of healing and willing to put in the required effort, recovery is achievable.

Forgiving Infidelity, Adultery, Separation and Divorce

"Forgiveness possesses the strength to empower and liberate."

Maybe you have experienced betrayal from a spouse or partner, causing a rift in your relationship. Alternatively, you might have grown apart due to various factors, such as the pressures and difficulties of contemporary life, leading to a separation from your significant other. Alternatively, you might have undergone, or still be going through, a tumultuous and distressing divorce.

This can be an extremely agonizing and solitary encounter, leaving you unsure if there is any chance of resolving the situation with your partner. Despite hoping for a positive outcome, the fear of the opposite may weigh heavily on you. Nevertheless, it is unnecessary to exacerbate the already difficult situation. By being open to forgiveness, much of the pain and suffering can be relinquished.

Forgiveness is not synonymous with accepting someone back into our lives. Instead, it serves as a tool to relinquish the pain from a situation so that we may determine the best course of action. When someone we love betrays our trust, whether it be through infidelity, unfaithfulness, adultery, or extramarital sex, we can experience an intense emotional shock that feels comparable to losing a loved one to death. This sense of loss is due to the realization that everything we envisioned and planned with that person is now in jeopardy or has been destroyed. We grieve not only for what has been lost but also for what could have been. This loss may even include the betrayal of losing a best friend in addition to a lover. At times, we may question whether we can ever trust someone again or become inclined to become bitter and cynical.

Despite the overwhelming pain and loss, there is still a way forward. We have the power to choose our path towards happiness and fulfillment. We may question how to move on from the pain and ask ourselves if we should forgive the person who caused us harm. However, it is essential not to allow our anger, bitterness, and resentment to consume us as it will only further worsen the situation. Instead, we can learn to heal from the pain caused by infidelity and adultery in ways that enhance our wisdom and resilience.

Forgiveness and reconciliation are two separate concepts that should not be confused with each other.

It's essential to recognize that forgiveness and reconciliation, while often linked, are not interchangeable. 'Forgiveness' involves relinquishing the urge to punish someone, while 'reconciliation' involves repairing and maintaining a relationship with that person. It's possible to forgive without seeking reconciliation, meaning we can release the desire for punishment while still choosing not to remain in a relationship, or to establish a different type of relationship than before the offense. Forgiving and reconciling are two distinct choices.

It's advisable to focus on forgiving the other person before deciding on reconciliation. By forgiving them first, we can let go of painful emotions and ensure that any decision we make regarding reconciliation is clear, wise, and compassionate, rather than driven by bitterness, resentment, or anger. Making a decision about the relationship before forgiving the other person may lead us to act out of a desire for revenge, which could cause long-term harm to us as well.

Tough forgiveness:
The concept of Tough Forgiveness is an option that we may choose to adopt, akin to "tough love". This involves forgiving the person and working towards it, but with negotiated terms and conditions regarding the reconciliation process. Tough Forgiveness entails establishing explicit agreements with the individual about acceptable and unacceptable behavior. However, we approach this with mutual respect, rather than as a form of emotional manipulation or subtle retaliation.

Self-forgiveness:
In the aftermath of relationship difficulties, we often find ourselves shouldering the blame, questioning our actions with self-doubt and a sense

of failure. This is where the concept of Self Forgiveness becomes crucial, as it's all too easy to oscillate between blaming ourselves and blaming the other person. Blame is not constructive; instead, we need to cultivate compassion and understanding towards both ourselves and the other individual. To achieve this, we must practice self-forgiveness and extend forgiveness to the other person. Forgiving ourselves is integral to forgiving the other person, and vice versa. This is the nature of forgiveness; it grows by giving.

How to Forgive:

The most crucial aspect to consider is "How do we forgive?" or "How do I forgive?" Many individuals are taught that they ought to forgive, yet they are not instructed on the 'how' of forgiveness. It's not surprising if you're unsure how to forgive since you were likely never taught how to do so.

However, there is a solution to this predicament. You can learn to forgive quickly and easily by utilizing the Four Steps to Forgiveness. This is a simple, practical technique that anyone can use, regardless of their philosophy, religion, or beliefs. It operates on basic principles that everyone can comprehend and put into practice. You do not have to hold any specific beliefs; all you have to do is apply the Four Steps and witness the results.

Step 1: Jot down the individuals whom you need to forgive and the reasons for which you need to forgive them.

Step 2: Create a record of the unhappy emotions you're currently experiencing regarding the situation. It's crucial that you list your genuine feelings rather than the ones you believe you "should" feel in a polite or amicable setting. To progress, you must start from where you are, not from where you want to be. Moving forward is only possible when you begin from where you genuinely are.

Step 3: Prepare a catalogue of the advantages you will receive by forgiving the situation. These advantages will frequently be the reverse of your current emotions. For example, sorrow may turn into joy, anger may transform into tranquility, and a sense of burden may become a feeling of lightness.

If you're unsure about the benefits, select a few general positive emotions that you'd like to experience as a starting point, such as "serenity," "liberation," "greater ease," "more self-assuredness," and so on. To assist you in visualizing how much better you will feel once you have forgiven, imagine the benefits.

Step 4: Create a Forgiveness Affirmation that includes the benefits you listed in Step 3 that resonate with you the most at the moment. This involves acknowledging who you plan to forgive and recognizing the advantages that arise from forgiving them. Repeat this sentence slowly in your mind at least three times and then return to Step 1. Keep repeating the process until you feel a sense of relief.

Forgiving others leads to an increase in happiness due to the following reasons.

When you forgive:

i. You release the pain of the past and let go of bitter, resentful, and angry feelings that may be clouding your life.

ii. You give yourself the freedom to either stay in the situation without feeling bitterness and resentment, or to leave it without feeling shame or guilt. If you choose to leave, it's not out of revenge, but rather from the clarity that the situation is not contributing to your happiness.

iii. You can grow in wisdom from what you've gained from the person or situation. Your mind is not cluttered by unhappy feelings, allowing you to see the ways you've learned and grown, which can contribute to your sense of happiness and wellbeing.

iv. You realize that you are freer within yourself and less likely to create similar situations because you've allowed yourself to grow from your experience instead of being diminished by it.

v. As you judge other people less harshly and feel more kindly towards them, you'll also judge yourself less harshly and become kinder towards yourself.

vi. If you resent others because they have more than you, you'll block them from being able to help you. By releasing those resentful feelings, you'll be better able to create healthier personal and business relationships with people who can mentor you and assist you in achieving your goals.

In conclusion, forgiveness is a powerful tool that can bring many benefits to our lives. It allows us to let go of negative emotions, free ourselves from situations that no longer serve us, grow in wisdom, and create better relationships with others. Forgiveness also allows us to be kinder to ourselves and less judgmental towards others. It may not be easy to forgive, but with practice and the right techniques, such as the Four Steps to Forgiveness, it is possible to forgive quickly and easily. So, let us embrace forgiveness and experience the happiness and peace it brings to our lives.

Printed in the USA
CPSIA information can be obtained
at www.ICGtesting.com
LVHW020208081124
796062LV00010B/372